HAVE A GOOD AND GODLY DAY

Words of Wisdom on Pleasing God

WOODROW KROLL

BACK TO THE BIBLE
Lincoln, NE 68501

The excerpts in this book are from books
copyrighted by Woodrow Kroll and from his
messages on the *Back to the Bible* radio program.

All Scripture quotations are
from the Holy Bible, New King James Version.
Copyright © 1982 by Thomas Nelson, Inc.

HAVE A GOOD AND GODLY DAY
Copyright © 1996
The Good News Broadcasting Association, Inc.
All rights reserved.

From eternity's point of view, it's more important that we have a godly day than a good one. You can have a godly day even if you don't have a good day, but you can never really have a good day if it isn't also a godly day.

"This is the day which the LORD has made; we will rejoice and be glad in it."
Psalm 118:24

The cornerstone of the Christian faith is the resurrection of Jesus Christ.

*"I am the resurrection and the life. He who believes in Me,
though he may die, he shall live."*
John 11:25

Forgiveness is not an emotional response
to being hurt. Forgiveness is not rationalizing.
And forgiveness is not just forgetting about it.
To forgive means to cancel a debt.
It is a choice.

*"Be kind to one another, tenderhearted, forgiving one another,
just as God in Christ also forgave you."*
Ephesians 4:32

As long as you remain pliable in God's hand,
it's possible for your life to be remolded
and reshaped by God.
It's only when your life hardens like hardened
clay that you're begging to be cast aside into
the potter's field.

*"And the vessel that he made of clay was marred in the hand of the potter; so he
made it again into another vessel, as it seemed good to the potter to make."*
Jeremiah 18:4

A family is meant to be a picture in miniature of what God's family is to be. We must put our every effort into making our families a foretaste of heaven.

"For if a man does not know how to rule his own house, how will he take care of the church of God?"
1 Timothy 3:5

The Savior demands complete loyalty, complete devotion—the type of loyalty that is so strong, so unswerving, that every other attachment becomes subject to it.

"Whoever desires to come after Me, let him deny himself, and take up his cross, and follow Me."
Mark 8:34

The challenge of the '90s is living a Christian life in a post-Christian world. Christ's light must now shine through our lives, and the deeper the darkness, the brighter that light must be.

"Do all things without murmuring and disputing, that you may become blameless and harmless, children of God without fault in the midst of a crooked and perverse generation, among whom you shine as lights in the world."
Philippians 2:14-15

The most important factor in true worship to God is a broken and contrite heart, a humble and steadfast spirit.

"Create in me a clean heart, O God, and renew a steadfast spirit within me."
Psalm 51:10

Every day each of us faces choices, just as Abraham and Lot did. Abraham chose to walk in faith and honor with God. Lot chose to walk in foolishness and dishonor. You're faced with those same choices today.

"Choose for yourselves this day whom you will serve, whether the gods which your fathers served that were one the other side of the River, or the gods of the Amorites, in whose land you dwell. But as for me and my house, we will serve the LORD."
Joshua 24:15

Take comfort today in the fact that when
you are burdened, when you are anxious,
you are loved. You are the object
of God's tender care.

*"The eternal God is your refuge,
and underneath are the everlasting arms."*
Deuteronomy 33:27

When Jesus is Lord of your life, He'll also be Lord of your decision-making process.

"But why do you call Me 'Lord, Lord,' and do not do the things which I say?"
Luke 6:46

There's no more risky time in life than when things are going well for us. That's when we are most susceptible to the attacks of Satan.

"Therefore let him who thinks he stands take heed lest he fall."
1 Corinthians 10:12

As branches, we must surrender to the will of the Vine or we'll be wild branches, fruitless branches, worthless branches.

"I am the true vine, and My Father is the vinedresser.
Every branch in Me that does not bear fruit He takes away; and
every branch that bears fruit He prunes, that it may bear more fruit."
John 15:1-2

When sin is not followed by repentance,
it will surely be followed by judgment.

*"For the LORD knows the way of the righteous, but the way
of the ungodly shall perish."*
Psalm 1:6

God has given us the Bible as a road map to heaven, a guide to living before we get there, and an autobiography to help us get to know Him more intimately.

"Your word is a lamp to my feet and a light to my path."
Psalm 119:105

Whatever you do, choose a Bible and use the one you choose. Dust on the Bible reflects dust in the heart. So don't just buy a Bible; know it in your head, stow it in your heart, and show it in your life.

"But his delight is in the law of the LORD,
and in His law he meditates day and night."
Psalm 1:2

The heart is the home of praise, not the lips.

"I will praise You, O LORD, with my whole heart;
I will tell of all Your marvelous works."
Psalm 9:1

God has given you reasoning powers, an ability to think through things in your life. You can use those reasoning powers to discern His will, because God's will is logical and reasonable.

"Therefore do not be unwise,
but understand what the will of the Lord is."
Ephesians 5:17

Faith is confidence in the righteous
character of God that fosters trust and hope
even when our circumstances foster
doubt and despair.

*"I will lift up my eyes to the hills—from whence comes my help?
My help comes from the LORD, who made heaven and earth."*
Psalm 121:1-2

The Bible says there is a wisdom that comes only from God. This godly wisdom is not gained by experience in the world. It's not learned by a book in a classroom. It's imparted to us by the Spirit of God.

"If any of you lacks wisdom, let him ask of God, who gives to all liberally and without reproach, and it will be given to him."
James 1:5

We miss the whole point of the Gospel
if we think it's a story about Jesus.
It isn't. The Gospel is Jesus.

"In the beginning was the Word, and the Word was with God,
and the Word was God."
John 1:1

Everything we do and say has
to be judged against some standard.
The Bible is that standard.

"All Scripture is given by inspiration of God, and is profitable for doctrine, for reproof, for correction, for instruction in righteousness, that the man of God may be complete, thoroughly equipped for every good work."
2 Timothy 3:16-17

When we live self-centered lives we are
denied the joy of delighting in others.

*"Be kindly affectionate to one another with brotherly love,
in honor giving preference to one another."*
Romans 12:10

The knowledge that God's grace is waiting
in the wings is insufficient grounds for
contemplating foolish action.
As Abraham finally learned, every friend of
God must carefully guard against even slight
lapses into the folly of sin.

*"Knowing this, that our old man was crucified with Him, that the body of sin
might be done away with, that we should no longer be slaves of sin."*
Romans 6:6

When man views his own circumstances,
he is given to despair; when he views God's
deliverance, he is given to praise.
The difference is his vision of God.

"Because You have been my help,
therefore in the shadow of Your wings I will rejoice."
Psalm 63:7

The secret of a faithful prayer life is not to spend our time foolishly fretting about the storms that surround our ship but, having taken note of the storms, to commit our ship to the great Captain of the seas. It is not the severity of the storm that is important, but the capability of the Captain.

"Then they cry out to the LORD in their trouble, and He brings them out of their distresses. He calms the storm, so that its waves are still."
Psalm 107:28-29

God never leaves His people alone, without a witness or guide. Living by faith sometimes means walking in the dark, but it never means living without a light.

"The people who walked in darkness have seen a great light; those who dwelt in the land of the shadow of death, upon them a light has shined."
Isaiah 9:2

The clouds of concern may completely encircle us today, but God will remove them in His own good time and will provide direction for us if we simply trust Him and wait upon Him.

"Rest in the LORD, and wait patiently for Him; do not fret because of him who prospers in his way."
Psalm 37:7

Persistence in doing what is right always
brings the prosperity of God.

*"And let us not grow weary while doing good,
for in due season we shall reap if we do not lose heart."*
Galatians 6:9

Two things must never be underestimated in this life. The first is the love of God; the second is the influence of a mother's prayer.

"In this the love of God was manifested toward us, that God has sent His only begotten Son into the world, that we might live through Him."
1 John 4:9

Satisfaction for the soul cannot be found
apart from fellowship with the Lord.

*"That I may know Him and the power of His resurrection, and the
fellowship of His sufferings, being conformed to His death."*
Philippians 3:10

When our souls thirst for the Lord as our parched tongues thirst for water, when our appetite for righteousness equals our appetite for food, then we will make it a habit of rising early in the morning to make our first appointment of the day an appointment with God.

"As the deer pants for the water brooks, so pants my soul for You, O God. My soul thirsts for God, for the living God."
Psalm 42:1-2

The Master rose up early to seek a solitary place to pray. As tired as He must have been, the Lord would allow nothing to interfere with His practice of rising early and praying alone.

"Now in the morning, having risen a long while before daylight,
He went out and departed to a solitary place; and there He prayed."
Mark 1:35

Covenant with God that you will rise early
in the morning to seek His face in prayer.
You won't believe the difference in how
your day goes.

"O God, You are my God; early will I seek you."
Psalm 63:1

Prayer works best when nothing else works at all. When the situation is hopeless, prayer fosters hope.

"Hear me when I call, O God of my righteousness! You have relieved me when I was in distress; have mercy on me, and hear my prayer."
Psalm 4:1

Each of us possesses different gifts
and abilities, but none of us is unimportant
in the work of the Lord.

*"For as we have many members in one body, but all the members do not
have the same function, so we, being many, are one body in Christ, and
individually members of one another."*
Romans 12:4-5

There is a freshness and charm about early morning praises that cannot be matched at any other hour of the day. Praise the Lord early and you will praise Him well.

"It is good to give thanks to the LORD, and to sing praises to Your name, O Most High; to declare Your lovingkindness in the morning, and Your faithfulness every night."
Psalm 92:1-2

True obedience neither procrastinates
nor questions.

*"I must work the works of Him who sent Me while it is day;
the night is coming when no one can work."*
John 9:4

The believer in Christ doesn't have a new lease on life; he has an entirely new life.

"Therefore, if anyone is in Christ, he is a new creation; old things have passed away; behold, all things have become new."
2 Corinthians 5:17

The greatest hindrance to answered prayer
is personal, unconfessed sin.

*"But your iniquities have separated you from your God; and your
sins have hidden His face from you, so that He will not hear."*
Isaiah 59:2

When the plans of men are in conflict
with the purposes of God,
they are destined for defeat.

"The LORD brings the counsel of the nations to nothing;
He makes the plans of the peoples of no effect."
Psalm 33:10

Lingering at the door of sin is an open invitation to enter that door. We must flee temptation and the presence of evil if we would remain true to God.

"Flee also youthful lusts; but pursue righteousness, faith, love, peace with those who call on the Lord out of a pure heart."
2 Timothy 2:22

One of the greatest difficulties in being a soldier in the army of the Lord is to recognize that we are but soldiers on the field of battle and not generals in the war room. The battle is the Lord's, not ours.

"Thus says the LORD to you: 'Do not be afraid nor dismayed because of this great multitude, for the battle is not yours, but God's.'"
2 Chronicles 20:15

Occasions do arise when we must obey God rather than men. That to which we are subjected because of our stand for Christ is not our concern. Our concern is that we take the stand.

"Watch, stand fast in the faith, be brave, be strong."
1 Corinthians 16:13

If we enjoyed the vantage point of heaven, above both space and time, we would readily see the hand of God guiding us through history.

"For this is God, our God forever and ever;
He will be our guide even to death."
Psalm 48:14

If we get our eyes off our problems and on their solution, off our circumstances and on the God who controls them, off ourselves and on Him, there's no telling what God will do for us.

"If then you were raised with Christ, seek those things which are above, where Christ is, sitting at the right hand of God. Set your mind on things above, not on things on the earth."
Colossians 3:1-2

To live in God's permissive will is but to receive temporary blessing. Saul was Israel's choice; Jesus is God's choice. How much better off we are to live in His perfect will rather than to settle for His permissive will.

"As for God, His way is perfect; the word of the LORD is proven; He is a shield to all who trust in Him."
Psalm 18:30

The same God who has the power
to shake the heavens also has the power to
make unshakable His Word.

*"The grass withers, the flower fades,
but the word of our God stands forever."*
Isaiah 40:8

When we inform God of our situation in prayer, it is not because He is unaware of how desperate we are; we do it so we are aware of how desperate we are.

"Be anxious for nothing, but in everything by prayer and supplication, with thanksgiving, let your requests be made known to God."
Philippians 4:6

While God's mercies may not always be
visible, they are always present. The mercies
of God may change their form, as the morning
light varies from the evening light,
but the mercies of God will never cease
to give their light.

"For the LORD is good; His mercy is everlasting,
and His truth endures to all generations."
Psalm 100:5

God adapts His mercy to our immediate needs each day. His mercies are not chiseled in stone but are vital and vibrant.

"Through the LORD'S mercies we are not consumed, because His compassions fail not. They are new every morning; great is Your faithfulness."
Lamentations 3:22-23

An unsatisfied life results from an unsurrendered will. Emptiness is the cup into which God pours blessing.

"If anyone desires to come after Me, let him deny himself, and take up his cross, and follow Me. For whoever desires to save his life will lose it, and whoever loses his life for My sake will find it."
Matthew 16:24-25

Incomplete obedience is the half-brother of disobedience. Not to obey God explicitly is to disobey Him implicitly.

"'Obey My voice, and do according to all that I command you; so shall you be My people, and I will be your God.'"
Jeremiah 11:4

We must never shy away from impossible situations. When the odds seem least favorable for our success, that is when God can gain the greatest glory.

"'For with God nothing will be impossible.'"
Luke 1:37

The Lord calls to each of us to "come and dine," and if we are to be an effective and useful tool in the Master's hand we must find our feet under His table frequently.

"You prepare a table before me in the presence of my enemies;
You anoint my head with oil; my cup runs over."
Psalm 23:5

There are no small people,
small tasks or small responsibilities
in the service of God.

*"But God has chosen the foolish things of the world to put to
shame the wise; and God has chosen the weak things of the
world to put to shame the things which are mighty."*
1 Corinthians 1:27

When the nipping north winds of calamity chill our nights and cause us to be restless, we may rest in the promise of God that "weeping may endure [only] for a night." God always places a time limit on the suffering and restlessness of His children.

"Blessed is the man who endures temptation; for when he has been proved, he will receive the crown of life which the Lord has promised to those who love Him."
James 1:12

We may be sure that no physician ever weighed out medicine to his patients with half as much care and exactness as God weighs out the trials of a sleepless night to us. Morning will come, and with it God's promised joy.

"For His anger is but for a moment, His favor is for life; weeping may endure for a night, but joy comes in the morning."
Psalm 30:5

We must never be ashamed to confess
that we have failed, for this is but one way
of saying we are wiser today than
we were yesterday.

*"Not that I have already attained, or am already perfected; but I press on,
that I may lay hold of that for which Christ Jesus has also laid hold of me."*
Philippians 3:12

It is as much a part of the Christian's life
to know afflictions as it is to know mercies;
to know when God smites as to know
when He smiles.

*"In this you greatly rejoice, though now for a little while, if need be, you have been
grieved by various trials, that the genuineness of your faith, being much more precious
than gold that perishes, though it is tested by fire, may be found to praise, honor,
and glory at the revelation of Jesus Christ."*

1 Peter 1:6-7

Affliction tests character and character tested, with the right response, is character strengthened. Rejoice today that God loves you enough to afflict you.

"For our light affliction, which is but for a moment, is working for us a far more exceeding and eternal weight of glory."
2 Corinthians 4:17

We may never be able to understand fully the methods or motives of God, but we are not required to understand them, simply to trust them.

"Oh, the depth of the riches both of the wisdom and knowledge of God!
How unsearchable are His judgments and His ways past finding out!"
Romans 11:33

We should never attempt to walk alone throughout the day and to chart our own course when we have the ability to tap the resources of heaven in the morning and receive our marching orders for the day.

"Your ears shall hear a word behind you, saying, 'This is the way, walk in it,' whenever you turn to the right hand or whenever you turn to the left."
Isaiah 30:21

When we live lives that are pleasing
before the Lord, godly lives, righteous lives,
we may always be assured that no matter
where our steps take us, we have been led
there by the Lord God Himself.

*"The steps of a good man are ordered by the LORD,
and He delights in his way."*
Psalm 37:23

The ability to meet affliction with
an uncompromising endurance and
an unflinching respect for God is one of
the marks of true Christian character.

"Though He slay me, yet will I trust Him."
Job 13:15

The man who bows the lowest
in the presence of God stands the straightest
in the presence of sin.

*"Therefore God also has highly exalted Him and given Him the name which
is above every name, that at the name of Jesus every knee should bow, of
those in heaven, and of those on earth, and of those under the earth."*
Philippians 2:9-10

Lord, give me a task larger than myself,
wisdom greater than my years,
friends to share my vision,
sufficient funds to realize it and length
of days to accomplish it. Amen.

*"You have granted me life and favor,
and Your care has preserved my spirit."*
Job 10:12

If the largeness of one's heart is determined by the number of people for whom we genuinely care, how big God's heart must be.

"Casting all your care upon Him, for He cares for you."
1 Peter 5:7

The world may have many religions,
but it still has only one Savior.

"I, even I, am the LORD, and besides Me there is no savior."
Isaiah 43:11

If every Bible in the world gathering dust
was blown off at the same time, we'd all die
in the dust storm.

*"Let the wicked forsake his way, and the unrighteous man his thoughts;
let him return to the LORD, and He will have mercy on him; and to our
God, for He will abundantly pardon."*
Isaiah 55:7

If the president or prime minister entered my room I would most likely rise; if Jesus Christ entered my room I would most certainly kneel.

"'As I live, says the Lord, every knee shall bow to Me, and every tongue shall confess to God.'"
Romans 14:11

It is only after we have suffered the consequences of disobedience that we can appreciate the wisdom of obedience.

"Like an earring of gold and an ornament of fine gold is a wise reprover to an obedient ear."
Proverbs 25:12

The greatest degree of Christian harmony comes not when we simply accommodate one another, but when we genuinely appreciate one another.

"Beloved, if God so loved us, we also ought to love one another."
1 John 4:11

Faith is the father of conviction.

*"Let us hold fast the confession of our hope without wavering,
for He who promised is faithful."*
Hebrews 10:23

I am not driven by faith in what lies ahead of me or by faith in what lies within me, but by faith in the God who stands behind me.

"'Therefore know that the LORD your God, He is God, the faithful God who keeps covenant and mercy for a thousand generations with those who love Him and keep His commandments.'"

Deuteronomy 7:9

Sanctification is being the person of God
before doing the work of God.

"Be holy; for I am holy."
1 Peter 1:16

When we forgive one another as God forgave us, it won't bring revival in the church. It will be revival in the church.

"Bearing with one another, and forgiving one another, if anyone has a complaint against another; even as Christ forgave you, so you also must do."
Colossians 3:13

If you want to rule, learn to serve. If you want to lead, learn to follow. If you want to succeed, learn to make others succeed.

"Just as the Son of Man did not come to be served, but to serve, and to give His life a ransom for many."
Matthew 20:28

When we draw our final breath, the question will not be who we are but who we've been. Not how much we've got, but how much we've given. Not if we've won, but if we've run. Not if we were a success, but if we were a servant.

*"I have fought the good fight, I have finished the race,
I have kept the faith."*
2 Timothy 4:7

We do not measure our success as leaders by the number of people we lead, but by the number of people we serve.

"Whoever desires to become great among you,
let him be your servant."
Matthew 20:26

A good deal of criticism is heavily laden with envy.

"For where envy and self-seeking exist, confusion and every evil thing will be there."
James 3:16

Better to be criticized unjustly by people who are in error than to be criticized justly because you are yourself in error.

"Do not fear the reproach of men, nor be afraid of their revilings."
Isaiah 51:7

Blessing must be distinguished from possessing; otherwise, how could Job say, "The Lord gave, and the Lord hath taken away; blessed be the name of the Lord"?

"Not that I speak in regard to need, for I have learned in whatever state I am, to be content."
Philippians 4:11

Sometimes the best way to prove
you have a command of the language is
to say nothing.

*"To everything there is a season, a time for every purpose
under heaven: . . . a time to keep silence, and a time to speak."*
Ecclesiastes 3:1, 7

A Christian who carries a cross
on his shoulder will never have room
to carry a chip there.

*"But God forbid that I should glory except in the cross of our Lord Jesus
Christ, by whom the world has been crucified to me, and I to the world."*
Galatians 6:14

True repentance hates the sin more than
the penalty for sin.

"For godly sorrow produces repentance to salvation, not to be regretted."
2 Corinthians 7:10

The reason Satan so easily influences our children may be that he has so much influence over their parents.

"Do not love the world or the things in the world. If anyone loves the world, the love of the Father is not in him."
1 John 2:15

People with big hearts sympathize;
people with little hearts criticize.

*"'A good man out of the good treasure of his heart brings forth good;
and an evil man out of the evil treasure of his heart brings forth evil.
For out of the abundance of the heart his mouth speaks.'"*
Luke 6:45

The difference between a rumor
and Turkish coffee is that one has
no grounds.

*"Finally, brethren, whatever things are true, whatever things are noble,
whatever things are just, whatever things are pure, whatever things are
lovely, whatever things are of good report, if there is any virtue and if
there is anything praiseworthy—meditate on these things."*
Philippians 4:8

Our greatest enemy is fear
that paralyzes faith.

*"For God has not given us a spirit of fear, but of power and of
love and of a sound mind."*
2 Timothy 1:7

Great prayers are an explosive mix of passion and preparation. We need to know what to pray for and how to pray.

"The effective, fervent prayer of a righteous man avails much."
James 5:16

We wander from godliness
not so much by becoming adulterous
or idolatrous but simply by forgetting
the things that please the Lord.

"My son, do not forget my law, but let your heart keep my commands."
Proverbs 3:1

Do what it takes to be empowered to pray.
Pull over, stand still, hang up, hit the
off button—do whatever is necessary to take
a seat and talk with God.

*"'But you, when you pray, go into your room, and when you have shut
your door, pray to your Father who is in the secret place; and your Father
who sees in secret will reward you openly.'"*
Matthew 6:6

The foundation of godliness
is a recognition of who God is
and who we are.

*"What is man that You are mindful of him,
and the son of man that You visit him?"*
Psalm 8:4

The ease with which we confess sin may be a clue to the genuineness of our confession. If we find it too easy, it may also be too shallow.

"Draw near to God and He will draw near to you. Cleanse your hands, you sinners; and purify your hearts, you double-minded. Lament and mourn and weep! Let your laughter be turned to mourning and your joy to gloom."

James 4:8-9

You have a choice between humanistic
self-esteem or imputed righteousness.
Take the righteousness.
It will lead you all the way to heaven.

*"Then the righteous will shine forth as the sun in the
kingdom of their Father."*
Matthew 13:43

Forgiveness is an act of the will.
It's a choice.
It's not an emotional response to a situation;
it is a volitional response to a person.

"'For if you forgive men their trespasses,
your heavenly Father will also forgive you.'"
Matthew 6:14

If God has the kind of character worth trusting, He has character worth trusting when the bills pile up, when the news from the doctor isn't good, when the enemy launches surprise attacks against us.

"For You have been a shelter for me, and a strong tower from the enemy. I will abide in Your tabernacle forever; I will trust in the shelter of Your wings."
Psalm 61:3-4

Empowered prayer always
comes back to faith.
Prayer that begins without faith
proceeds without power.

*"But without faith it is impossible to please Him, for he who
comes to God must believe that He is, and that He is a
rewarder of those who diligently seek Him."*
Hebrews 11:6

Prayer is not the privilege of the spiritual elite. Prayer is not for perfect people. Prayer is for people who have a need and a relationship with God that can fill that need.

"Come to Me, all you who labor and are heavy laden, and I will give you rest."
Matthew 11:28

God is omnipresent, yet as personal as if He were yours and yours alone. He is immense, yet small enough to fill your tender heart. He is allwise, yet invites you to tell Him what's on your mind.

"O LORD, You have searched me and known me. . . .
You comprehend my path and my lying down, and are acquainted
with all my ways."
Psalm 139:1, 3

Prayer is the preface to real purpose,
the prologue to God's power, the prelude
to personal peace and the precursor to
world evangelism.

"Continue earnestly in prayer, being vigilant in it with thanksgiving;
meanwhile praying also for us, that God would open to us a door
for the word, to speak the mystery of Christ."
Colossians 4:2-3

When the ministry of prayer is elevated, so is every other ministry. Preaching becomes better with prayer. Witnessing becomes more effective with prayer. Government becomes more just with prayer.

"If My people who are called by My name will humble themselves, and pray and seek My face, and turn from their wicked ways, then I will hear from heaven, and will forgive their sin and heal their land."
2 Chronicles 7:14

Prayer is a gift from God.
It's the one gift all Christians can
enjoy equally.

*"For the eyes of the LORD are on the righteous,
and his ears are open to their prayers."*
1 Peter 3:12

Men don't reject the Bible because it contradicts itself; they reject it because it contradicts them.

"For the message of the cross is foolishness to those who are perishing, but to us who are being saved it is the power of God."
1 Corinthians 1:18

Anything that doesn't square with the Bible, any doctrine that doesn't have the support of the Holy Scriptures, any lifestyle that is contrary to God's Word should find no home in the Christian's life.

"That we should no longer be children, tossed to and fro and carried about with every wind of doctrine. . . but, speaking the truth in love, may grow up in all things into Him who is the head—Christ."
Ephesians 4:14-15

You may not be able to understand
all you read in the Bible, but you can obey
all that you do understand.

"If you know these things, happy are you if you do them."
John 13:17

If you were the only person who ever lived on this planet, God still would have sent His Son to die just for you.

"I say to you that likewise there will be more joy in heaven over one sinner who repents than over ninety-nine just persons who need no repentance."
Luke 15:7

No sinner is too hardened that he or she
cannot be softened by the love of God.
No sinner is too sinful that he or she cannot
be forgiven by the mercy of God.

"Christ Jesus came into the world to save sinners, of whom I am chief."
1 Timothy 1:15

God did not stay in heaven and look at your difficulties. He came here to do something about them.

*"And the Word became flesh and dwelt among us,
and we beheld His glory, the glory as of the only begotten
of the Father, full of grace and truth."*
John 1:14

The death and resurrection of Jesus Christ
are not traced on our memories as much
as they are plowed into the soil of history.

*"'This Jesus God has raised up,
of which we are all witnesses.'"*
Acts 2:32

Sanctification is inward purity
before it is outward piety.

"Who may ascend into the hill of the LORD?
Or who may stand in His holy place?
He who has clean hands and a pure heart."
Psalm 24:3-4

We would never think of growing physically
by watching someone else eat; amazingly
we must think we can grow spiritually by
watching someone else read his Bible.

*"But grow in the grace and knowledge of our Lord
and Savior Jesus Christ."*
2 Peter 3:18

Most people don't come to Christ as the result of an argument; they come as the result of a testimony. Tell your friends what Christ has done for you. They can't argue with that.

"Come and hear, all you who fear God, and I will declare what He has done for my soul."
Psalm 66:16

Before he came to himself,
the Prodigal Son had a bright
future behind him.

"And he arose and came to his father. But when he was still a
great way off, his father saw him and had compassion,
and ran and fell on his neck and kissed him."
Luke 15:20

When it comes to service, God is more interested in our availability than our ability, more in our godliness than our gifts, more in our disposition than our position.

"For bodily exercise profits a little, but godliness is profitable for all things, having promise of the life that now is and of that which is to come."
1 Timothy 4:8

Responsibility allows us to make decisions;
freedom allows us to make wrong decisions;
wisdom allows us to make intelligent decisions;
but only character allows us to make right
decisions. It takes a lifetime to build character, but
a single moment of foolishness to destroy it.

"The foolishness of a man twists his way."
Proverbs 19:3

God is not looking for willing workers;
He's looking for busy workers.
He doesn't call those who will go,
but those who are going.

*"'Let your light so shine before men, that they may see your
good works and glorify your Father in heaven.'"*
Matthew 5:16

Nothing is so contagious
as discouragement.

"A merry heart makes a cheerful countenance, but by sorrow
of the heart the spirit is broken."
Proverbs 15:13

What we tolerate in our ears
is a good measure of what we will allow
to enter our hearts.

"And He said to them, 'Take heed what you hear.'"
Mark 4:24

While it is true that all truth is God's truth, it is not true that all of God's truth is equally important. We must give greater attention to God's eternal truth than to His temporal truth.

"The entirety of Your word is truth, and every one of Your righteous judgments endures forever."
Psalm 119:160

Many organs in the human body
are connected, but none with a stronger
tie than the heart and the tongue.

"A wholesome tongue is a tree of life,
but perverseness in it breaks the spirit."
Proverbs 15:4

When God moves in the hearts of men
and women to do great things for Him,
He gives them vision; but before that,
He gives them faith.

"For we walk by faith, not by sight."
2 Corinthians 5:7

Children learn value by the amount of money we give them. That's why we should never send them off to the mall with more money that we send them off to church.

"For the love of money is a root of all kinds of evil, for which some have strayed from the faith in their greediness, and pierced themselves through with many sorrows."
1 Timothy 6:10

It was Abraham's faith to act that proved the presence of his faith, but it was his act of faith that proved its quality.

"He [Abraham] did not waver at the promise of God through unbelief, but was strengthened in faith, giving glory to God, and being fully convinced that what He had promised He was able to perform."
Romans 4:20-21

God's heroes are not those who make
a public confession of sin. God's heroes are
those who have no need of confession.

"Blessed are the pure in heart,
for they shall see God."
Matthew 5:8

So much of our future
is unclaimed because of the
false strength we draw from the past.

*"But one thing I do, forgetting those things which are behind
and reaching forward to those things which are ahead,
I press toward the goal for the prize of the
upward call of God in Christ Jesus."*
Philippians 3:13-14

Satan is a liar. When he speaks a lie,
he is original. When he speaks the truth,
he plagiarizes.

*"'When he [Satan] speaks a lie, he speaks from his own
resources, for he is a liar and the father of it.'"*
John 8:44

God's love for us wasn't blind.
He saw us as dirty, greedy and unlovely.
But His love saw beyond the dirt
to our hurt, beyond the greed to our need,
beyond the unloveliness to our helplessness.

"But God demonstrates His own love toward us, in that while
we were still sinners, Christ died for us."
Romans 5:8

Obedient love is not just love that obeys,
but love that loves to obey. Obedient love is
not merely submissive love, but rather love
that relishes submission to the right person.

*"'You shall love the LORD your God will all your heart, with
all your soul, and with all your might.'"*
Deuteronomy 6:5

If we Christians spent as much time in prayer as we do watching the news, maybe we'd change the news.

"The end of all things is at hand; therefore be serious and watchful in your prayers."
1 Peter 4:7

True success is
the willingness to be considered
a failure by everyone but God.

*"'For the Lord does not see as man sees; for man looks at the
outward appearance, but the Lord looks at the heart.'"*
1 Samuel 16:7

What I suffer finds its meaning in why I suffer. If I suffer for the sake of my Savior, what I suffer is of little consequence.

"But rejoice to the extent that you partake of Christ's sufferings, that when His glory is revealed, you may also be glad with exceeding joy."
1 Peter 4:13

Do not fear the strength of external temptation to sin; fear rather the weakness of your internal determination to resist.

"Watch and pray, lest you enter into temptation. The spirit indeed is willing, but the flesh is weak."
Matthew 26:41

Never let a day go by
that you fail to thank God
for saving you.

*"I will render praises to You, for You have delivered
my soul from death."*
Psalm 56:12-13

Time is eternity's creating room, not eternity's waiting room.

*"But, beloved, do not forget this one thing,
that with the Lord one day is as a thousand years,
and a thousand years as one day."*
2 Peter 3:8

Every satanic attack on God's people is,
in reality, a heavenly battle fought
on an earthly battlefield.
We are not under attack. God is!

*"For we do not wrestle against flesh and blood,
but against principalities, against powers, against the rulers
of the darkness of this age, against spiritual hosts of
wickedness in the heavenly places."*
Ephesians 6:12

Trying times are not the time
to stop trying.

*"He gives power to the weak,
and to those who have no might
He increases strength."*
Isaiah 40:29

When you're at the end of your rope,
you'd better know who is holding
the other end.

*"In my distress I cried to the LORD,
and He heard me."*
Psalm 120:1

The search for significance is the most significant search of mankind. But if our significance is found in insignificant things, our search is itself insignificant.

"But seek first the kingdom of God and His righteousness, and all these things shall be added to you."
Matthew 6:33

Impatience is a greater impediment
to wisdom than ignorance.

*"But let patience have its perfect work, that you may be
perfect and complete, lacking nothing."*
James 1:4

Wisdom is a skillful approach to living, an approach to life that filters every experience we have through the fear of the Lord and the pages of His Word.

"Who is wise and understanding among you?
Let him show by good conduct that his works are done
in the meekness of wisdom."
James 3:13

Stewardship is not about paying dues.
It's not about paying bills. It's about
deliberately making deposits of time
and energy into God's eternal business.

*"He has put eternity in their hearts, except that no one can
find out the work that God does from beginning to end."*
Ecclesiastes 3:11

Couples today need spiritual bonding,
and the best glue in any marriage
is the Holy Spirit.

*"'But the Helper, the Holy Spirit, whom the Father will send
in My name, He will teach you all things, and bring to your
remembrance all things that I said to you.'"*
John 14:26

Love means we accept our friends'
imperfections, but it does not mean
we tolerate their sin.

*"Then I will teach transgressors Your ways,
and sinners shall be converted to You."*
Psalm 51:13

Hurtful words sometimes come
dressed in helpful robes.

"Blows that hurt cleanse away evil,
as do stripes the inner depths of the heart."
Proverbs 20:30

Trusting God is a strange thing.
We have a hard time bringing ourselves
to do it, and yet when there's nothing
else left, it always works.

"Believe in the LORD your God, and you shall be established;
believe His prophets, and you shall prosper."
2 Chronicles 20:20

Trusting ourselves and our wisdom
is the first inclination of humanity
and the last refuge of failure.

*"Trust in the LORD with all your heart,
and lean not on your own understanding."*
Proverbs 3:5

Success without prayer is
success without substance. It is an illusion,
a bubble floating toward a waiting pin.

*"Therefore I say to you, whatever things you ask when you
pray, believe that you receive them, and you will have them."*
Mark 11:24

We do not study the Bible to become
Bible students; Bible study must always
translate into service.

*"Be diligent to present yourself approved to God,
a worker who does not need to be ashamed,
rightly dividing the word of truth."*
2 Timothy 2:15

If success in prayer depended on how close you are to God, how close would be close enough? The distance between a holy God and sinful people is so great it cannot be perceptibly calibrated.

"For there is one God and one Mediator between God and men, the Man Christ Jesus."
1 Timothy 2:5

Those who fail to pray because
they do not feel close to God may not
feel close to God because they fail to pray.

*"Draw near to God
and He will draw near to you."*
James 4:8

Godly living means no regrets about yesterday, no embarrassments today, no schemes for tomorrow.

"For our boasting is this: the testimony of our conscience that we conducted ourselves in the world in simplicity and godly sincerity, not with fleshly wisdom but by the grace of God."
2 Corinthians 1:12